apartment living is great

An Exhibition by Lesley Marlene Siegel

Outré Gallery, Melbourne
July 2003

hand numbered limited edition exhibition catalog

this catalog is no. 1911 of 1965 copies

(with a special signed edition numbered between 1-25)

Outré Gallery Press

Interview with LESLEY MARLENE SIEGEL by GEMMA JONES

"Once you 'got' Pop, you could never see a sign the same way again. And once you thought Pop, you could never see America the same way again." – Andy Warhol

For those of us who don't know – can you explain the dingbat as a concept and a form?

A dingbat, in simple terms, is a 1960's era multi-level boxy style apartment building. They often have an exposed carport, or open garage with storage units facing the street, resting on "stilts," or beams in the front. The building façades are either left plain, which I refer to as "deprived dingbats," or adorned with a name in the form or a sign affixed to the front, or other decorative ornamentation, such as sconces, lights or grillwork.

How is this particularly Californian?

I actually think the dingbat is particularly "Southern Californian." Since we have a mild climate here, the buildings don't have to withstand harsh winters. So, a dingbat could be made of low-cost building materials, making them relatively inexpensive to produce, while at the same time affordable to renters. Even though I have seen dingbats in other parts of the state, I don't believe they are in such a high concentration as here in "SoCal."

What does it all say about local culture and personality?

I equate the Los Angeles dingbat apartment building with what our city is so famous for: the movie industry. As the dingbat apartment front is a clean stucco slate — a blank façade waiting for adornment — to me, it is equivalent to and symbolizes a movie theatre marquee. Once the letters of the signs are affixed, it calls out, not to moviegoers offering the film now playing, but to potential renters, offering a life inside a proposed mystical building that has been so exotically named.

All the wonderful apartment building names, quietly lining the streets of my hometown Los Angeles, to me, represent a secret language. They are hidden words waiting for their moment to be discovered, to have their "headshot" taken, and meet their mates as they play their role in the "Apartment Living is Great" series.

Describe your photo taking journey. Are you always armed with a camera "just in case", or do you go out on particular missions?

I don't actually carry a camera with me for the "just in case" moment of discovery, and yes, I definitely set out on intentional missions to shoot apartment building names.

In the early 1990's, I began a personal quest to photograph every single apartment building name that I could find. It started out rather casually, but as soon as I realized how many were out there, I set out on early morning treks, about 5:30a.m., and searched designated neighbourhoods. With my Mom, Shirley, on call for the early morning jaunts, my brother, Lewis, or my lifelong friend Celia for the not so early calls, we would methodically go up and down every single street of targeted neighbourhoods on a hunt for signage.

The early morning periods were best for a couple of reasons: since the sun was not directly overhead, there were less shadows, and there were less people out at that time of day.

In the different neighbourhoods we combed, my Mom and I would laughingly call certain streets either "user-hostile" or "user-friendly," depending on what kind of people were hanging out on them.

Have you ever been stopped from taking a photo?

Luckily no, but when I did take a photograph, I needed to be as quick as possible. As you can tell by looking at my proof sheets, for the most part, I have only one single picture of each sign. To be able to photograph the signage, I had to get very close to the building itself, and to curious observers, it looked like I was trying to take a picture inside the window of someone's apartment. So, I'm sure I did alarm some tenants when they saw me pull up in my car, jump out with camera in hand aimed straight up at their building, get back in my car and speed off.

What inspired you to take up photography?

Signage! Strictly speaking, I didn't officially "take up" photography; it was more of an interest in the subject matter and my wanting to document it. A pivotal point was when I took a photography class, and had at that time taken only two pictures of apartment building names. I showed them in a class review and the teacher, Laura London, who has now become a close friend, said they were great. That incident started me in motion and when I ran into her about six months later, I told her that I now had over six hundred photographs! We now joke together, all these years and over two thousand photographs later, and say that Laura "created a monster."

Aside from the apartment photography project, what other artworks/artforms and projects have you pursued?

I am working on a couple other photographic series, detailing other elements of architectural design and different forms of advertising found in Southern California.

Years ago, I tried to start an anti "mini-mall" campaign, but it never took off. At one point, Los Angeles was being proliferated by unsightly corner strip malls with generic stores, and caused an uproar for people with a certain aesthetic taste. I designed a logo and wanted to start a t-shirt movement against these mini-malls, but now, we've all kind of come to accept their presence.

What inspires you day to day?

Living in Los Angeles, I am continually inspired by the wonderful architecture of the past in this city. Just driving through the streets, I am amazed at all the different styles of buildings we have here, all the detail, and all the craftsmanship of the older buildings, especially the Spanish style, which is my all-time favorite. I try to take different routes as often as I can, so I don't miss out on any hidden apartment building names pining away on a lonely dead-end street.

I heard you collect actual signs when you get the chance! What can you tell us about this?

Yes, over the years, as part of the "Apartment Living is Great" project, I have been able to collect actual signs from buildings that are either being renovated or torn down. It's all a matter of timing, because Los Angeles is infamous for tearing down buildings without a second thought. When I am fortuitous enough to actually see a building that is slated for demolition, or get a tip-off from someone else, it's a race against the clock. I start by tracking down the owner, then start my negotiations and finagling to get permission to take the sign down. Usually, they have absolutely no interest in the sign at all, and when I approach them, it may be the first time they've ever given it a thought. I've been lucky, and usually, after many calls and much explanation about my passion for apartment building names and the project, they acquiesce and give me the okay to take the sign.

What do you do with them? Is there anything interesting about the way they are made?

Some I have up in my apartment and others are stored in my garage. The signs are surprisingly light; I can always carry them myself once they are removed from the building by my trusted handyman, Jose, who, as my own personal "Signage Spiderman," has climbed many a wall for me, while I wait below as he hands me one letter at a time. Most often they are made of wood, but sometimes plastic. The colors of the signs are usually very plain and not at all flashy.

What's your own home like?

I do live in an apartment but not a dingbat, rather a "white castle-like structure", as it is referred to by my friend Hilary. One thing about dingbats is that they are usually smallish inside, and since my apartment is from the 1930's, I am lucky to have a gigantic living room that serves as my gallery, with my artwork and signage lining the walls.

You take photos of essentially old buildings from a particular period. Is there something about the passage of time that comes through or that particularly fascinates you?

It's interesting to me that the signage I document was created close to three or four decades ago, and when I discovered them years later, they are in various stages of condition. **When I see a building where the name remains intact, and not falling apart or missing letters, it signifies to me that somehow this particular sign has a strength and has been able to survive all these years.**

As time passes, and letters fall, never to be replaced, or signs are completely obscured by a tree or prolific shrubbery in the front of the building, the historical value of the signage decreases. This has been frustrating to me, as there are some signs I just can't shoot because of this uncooperative, but healthy greenery.

Years ago, I needed to photograph an interesting sign, the "Nahas Pagai," for one of my docu-history pieces. The builder, Mr. Nahas, created the word "Pagai" by combining his two granddaughters' first names: Pam and Gail = "Pagai." The sign itself was hidden behind shrubbery, so two willing friends helped me out by scaling the building plus a tenant's window, and while using garden rakes, pulled apart the shrubs for a quick second, so I could get the picture! Luckily, no police were called out during this surreptitious "photo shoot."

How are your images about fantasy?

The people responsible for naming these buildings had the freedom to dip into their own personal fantasies and name an apartment after themselves, their spouse, children, or any other exotic theme that appealed to them. As far as I know, there were no rules, regulations or "Apartment Building Name Approval Board"; so builders, management companies and owners had complete freedom to use their imaginations and come up with a fantasy imprint to be placed on the building façade for the rest of the world to see.

Funny enough, there is actually a building given the name "Fantasie". The creative spelling of the word here is perfect evidence of someone's own "fantasy".

Susan Sontag says that "photography actively promotes nostalgia" and if you also consider nostalgia to be a longing tied to the desire for "home" your project is in lots of different ways very nostalgic. What is your personal take on these ideas of nostalgia in your work and in contemporary life?

As soon as I have photographed an apartment building name, it could, the very next day be gone, or if a letter falls, appear as a completely new and unintended word. I know that many of the signs in my collection no longer exist, and I am more than likely the only person that has even thought of, or cared enough about the signage and the history behind the names, to take their picture.

I do feel a sense of nostalgia, knowing I have no control over what the future of these signs, that I find so unique and wonderful, will be. **The signs struggle to survive at the hands of unappreciative remodelers, developers, or corporate property managers acting as architectural plastic surgeons.** They lie in wait with pliers, ready to yank the name off the front of the building, as a quick and easy facelift to attract new renters. It's sad to think that a sign left as a legacy to a child or family member, is no longer in the care of the person who erected it as a loving tribute many years ago.

But do you think there is something particular about images of 'homes' per se that has a resonance with people?

There have been times when my work is first seen, that some people may initially mistake the apartment names as being from motels. While the signs are similar in style and even thematically to the commercial signage found on motels, knowing that every single one is the name of a residential building makes them that much more fascinating to me, and I hope, for the viewer.

Your photos have a kind of sadness to them. What do you think evokes a feeling like this?

If there is a perceived sadness by some, I can attribute it, perhaps, to the feeling of hope or optimism that I'm certain was the intent of these building namers, but now, in fact, may be looked upon as kitsch by the jaded.

Often, I come across signs with a letter or letters missing, creating confounding words for passerbyers. For example, one of the first buildings I ever shot was the "Hayworth House." At the time I originally shot it, all the letters were intact, but the "u" was coming off its hinge and was leaning over onto the "s", so my nickname for the building was "the U is askew." Now, years later, the "u" is completely off, and what's sad to me, is that the person who cared enough to create this sign, is most assuredly not involved with the building anymore, and there is no one presently there who cares enough to fix it, leaving tenants to reside in what has now become known as the "Hayworth Ho se."

What is it about photography that is important to you in your project and in your life as a photographer?

I love the power of being able to document landscape and community history with photography; **finding visual elements in the built environment, that are omnipresent in our daily lives, yet invisible to the masses.**

When I first started taking pictures of apartment building names, I had absolutely no idea how many were out there. What still astounds me, and others as well, is that I was able to find over 2,000, and that number will always grow.

The fact that I saw something in a unique way, and was able to create this personal project, is very fulfiling. To me, each sign is a precious gem, and I have so much fun linking them together, as pieces of a puzzle, not truly intended to go together, but making perfect sense when combined in my thematic groupings.

At the same time, I've also felt that I've discovered a secret and embedded Los Angeles language or lexicon.

I also like to think of "Apartment Living Is Great" as a whimsical gift to my hometown. Since I am a Los Angeles native, it makes my project so much more special to me on a personal level.

A lot of your works, especially through the way they have been paired, have a subtle, inherent humor. What place does humor have in your project? Why is humor important?

People may look at the signs I've chosen to photograph and find them humorous, even before I pair them, because it may seem outrageous to have given everyday apartment buildings such exotic and personalized names. I love coming up with name groupings that — on their own might have one distinct meaning — and when grouped with one another, take on an entirely new and humorous life of their own.

What are the weirdest signs you've come across?

The first one that comes to mind is "un X ld," which takes a few seconds to grasp, and then the ingeniousness of this name really comes out. For someone to think so highly of their building (or themselves!) to firstly, name it "unexcelled," and then to have created this cryptic and wonderful spelling, is fantastic to me. I also think that the building called "The Unique," along the same lines as "un X ld," is really something in its audacious boasting!

**"Quo Vadis"
"The Double D"
"Career"
"Quakertown Terrace"
"Ultra Encino" "Chii-Sai"
"A Taste of Honey" "Queen Monci"
"Nomar" "The Urbanna"
"Ka-Jan Apts" "Thirteen Thirteen"
"OK Chalet" "Tousi Manor"
"Shangri Lodge" and "Bras Armé"**

From a design and typographical point of view, what significance do the signs embody?

In addition to the names themselves, "Apartment Living is Great" embodies the vast and varied display and craftsmanship of so many wonderful fonts and typefaces created by the signmakers.

It's interesting to see how often the style of the font goes along with the name itself. Many of the tiki-themed signs have been crafted in a style that tries to emulate a tiki carving. Some of the more "prissy" signs, named for flowers or fancy places, have been given a thin and airy scripted font, and can appear to want to fly right off the building.

You are interested in combining photos to expand their meaning and impact. How do you think this happens? What are some of your favourite pairings?

Since I've looked at these signs many times over, natural pairings jump out at me, and just make sense as a perfect and novel way to present them. It's a fun challenge for me, and I'm continuously seeing the apartment names in new ways each time I look at them. Some of my favorite pairings are: "Melody" with "Do Re Mi" – "Sans Souci" with "La Bonne Vie" – "Malibu" with "The Newport" – "The Cinema" with "The Starlet"

I have a group of actual starlet representations, created by pairing: "Villa Grace" with "Monaco" – "Rita Apts" with "The Hayworth" – "Shirley Knolls" with "Temple View." Also included in these starlets is "Norma Jean Apts," but she stands alone.

How does your project reflect something of your own philosophy about life?

One thing I try to keep in mind throughout my own life is the importance of subjectivity, and how we react to situations and interact with other people we encounter. I can say that my subjectivity must have led me to notice these signs in my own way, seek them out in such massive quantity, and enable me put them back together in all that has become "Apartment Living is Great."

**"Sign, sign, everywhere a sign
Blockin' out the scenery, breakin' my mind
Do this, don't do that, can't you read the sign?
– *Signs* by Five Man Electrical Band (1971)**

All of the photographs in the catalog were taken by Lesley Marlene Siegel between 1991 and 2003 as part of her ongoing project titled "Apartment Living is Great" which is comprised of over 2,300 black and white photographs, shot with 35mm film.

the plates

Starfire / Starlite Terrace

Starlite
Terrace

Los Capri / Griffith Lanai

The Bachelors / The Pad

Coco palms
Palm Manor
Twin Palms
Orlando Palms
Royal Palms
4300
Colfax PALMS
Pearl Palm
THE PALMS

16950
Balboa
PALMS

Four
Palms

Delores
Palms
11933

Sea Palms
12319

the Sun
dial Palms

Twin
Palms

Riviera
PALMS

monica Palms
NO
PARKING

Haven Oaks / Riverside Palms

4332
Riverside
Palms

Taj Mahal / Bombay / The Calcutta

The Sands / Vegas Terrace / Stardust

THE
Calcutta
15034

5322
Vegas Terrace

STARDUST

Hi-Life / Stoner Apts.

The Crown / Tiara

El Matador / El Charro

Sea Side / The Surfside

The Jamaican / The Montego

The Ocean Aire Terrace / The Golden Mermaid

Tiki
Harbor Isle
Aloha Gardens
The Tahiti
Glenlani Tiki
KAHLUA
The Tropikia
2402
D
MANAGED BY
DITURI CO.
REALTORS
453-3341
Luau APTS.

KONA PALI
TRADE WINDS 
Kona 
Apts
THE 
Tropics
14219
TAHITIAN 
KALA WAI 
The 
Polynesian
1830
BALI

Hampshire House / Harratt Towers

The Continental / The Riviera

Thirteen Thirteen / Sixty Sixty Six

Riviera Villa / Villa Riviera

Villa
Riviera

Caribbean / The Bahamas Apts.

Tiki / Glenlani Tiki

Valleyheart Ambassador / Baron Manor

Tiki / Quiet Village

QUIET VILLAGE

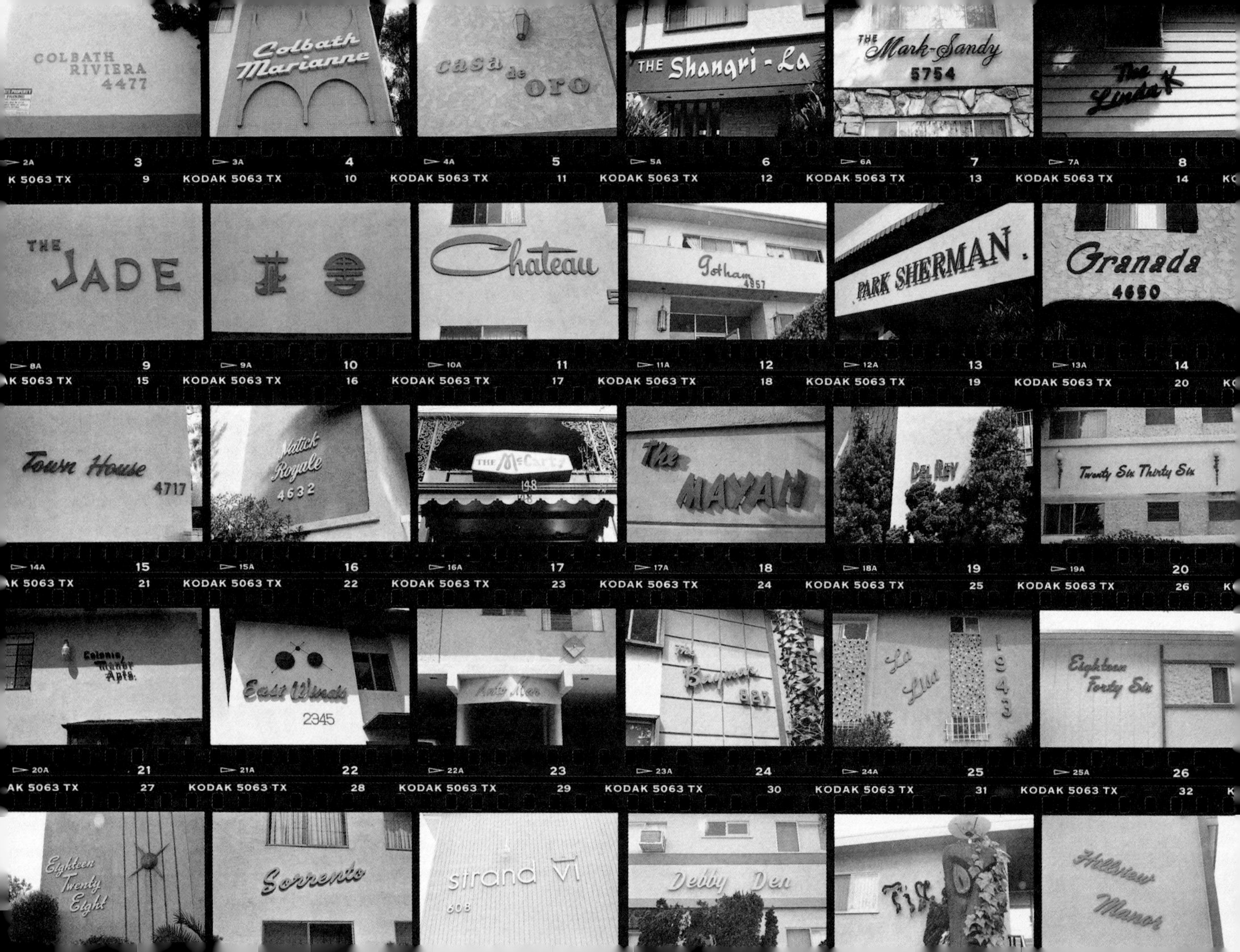

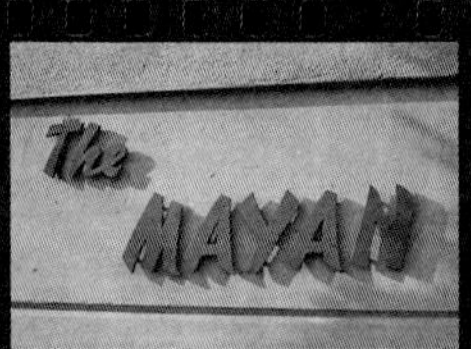

COLBATH
RIVIERA
4477
Colbath
Marianne
casa de oro
THE Shangri-La
THE Mark-Sandy
5754
The
2A 3
3A 4
4A 5
5A 6
6A 7
7A 8
K 5063 TX 9
KODAK 5063 TX 10
KODAK 5063 TX 11
KODAK 5063 TX 12
KODAK 5063 TX 13
KODAK 5063 TX 14
THE
JADE
Chateau
Gotham
PARK SHERMAN
Granada
4650
8A 9
9A 10
10A 11
11A 12
12A 13
13A 14
AK 5063 TX 15
KODAK 5063 TX 16
KODAK 5063 TX 17
KODAK 5063 TX 18
KODAK 5063 TX 19
KODAK 5063 TX 20
Town House
4717
Natick
Royale
4632
THE McCarty
148
The
MAYAN
Del Rey
Twenty Six Thirty Six
14A 15
15A 16
16A 17
17A 18
18A 19
19A 20
AK 5063 TX 21
KODAK 5063 TX 22
KODAK 5063 TX 23
KODAK 5063 TX 24
KODAK 5063 TX 25
KODAK 5063 TX 26
Colonia
Manor
Apts.
East Winds
2345
The
La
Lisa
1943
Eighteen
Forty Six
20A 21
21A 22
22A 23
23A 24
24A 25
25A 26
AK 5063 TX 27
KODAK 5063 TX 28
KODAK 5063 TX 29
KODAK 5063 TX 30
KODAK 5063 TX 31
KODAK 5063 TX 32
Eighteen
Twenty
Eight
Sorrento
strand VI
608
Debby Den
Hillview
Manor

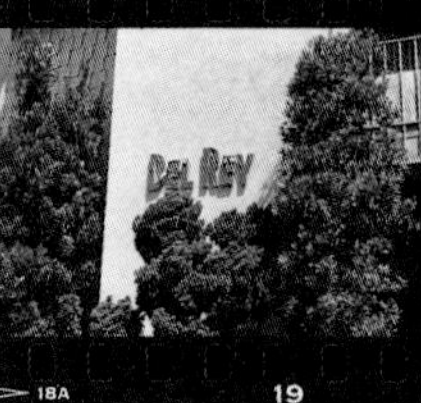

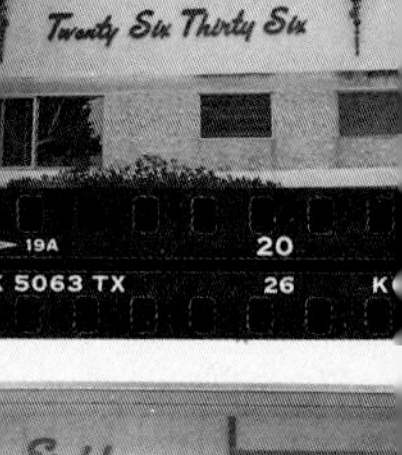

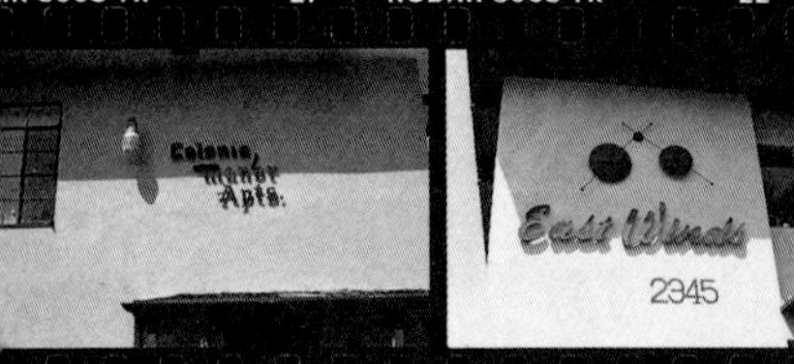

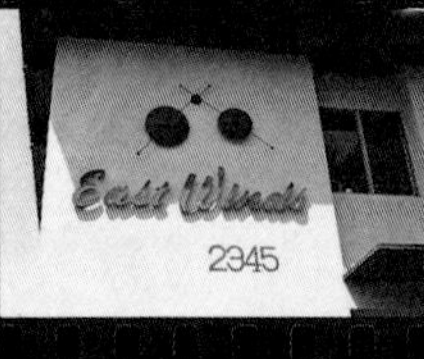

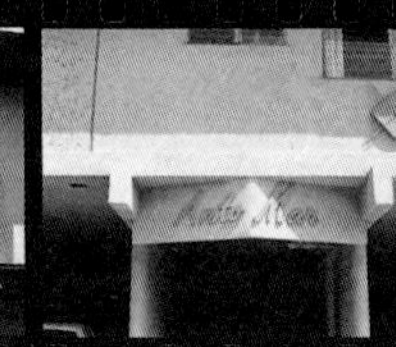

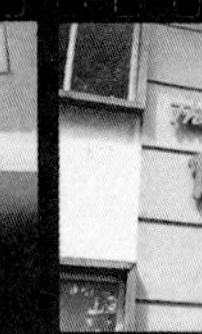

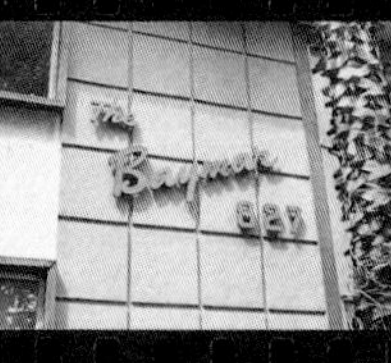

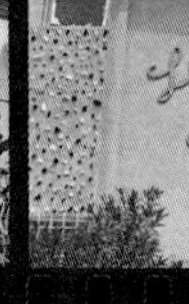

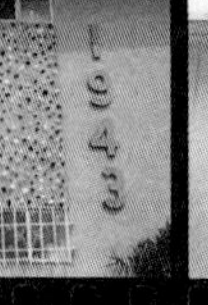

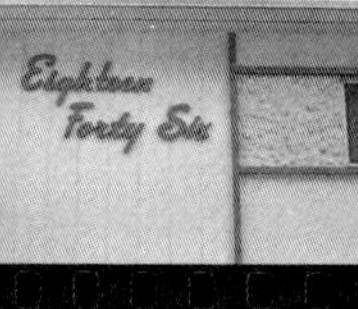

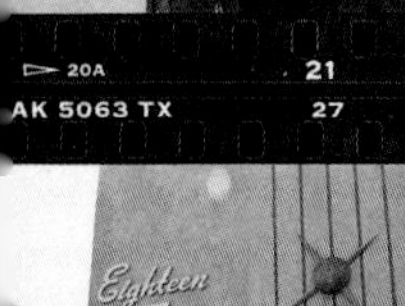

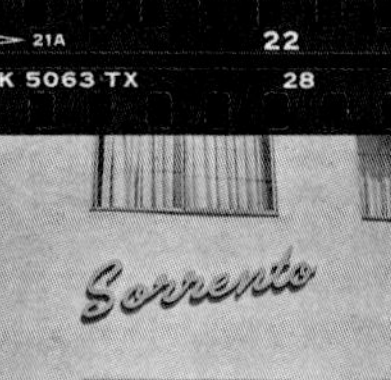

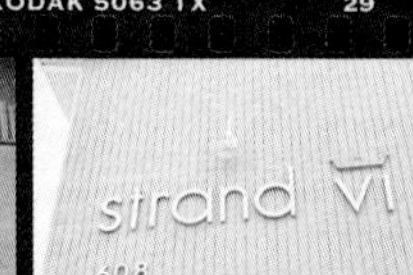

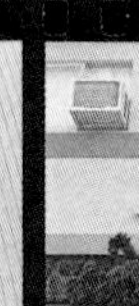

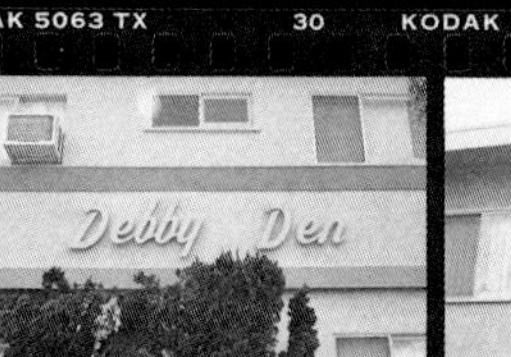

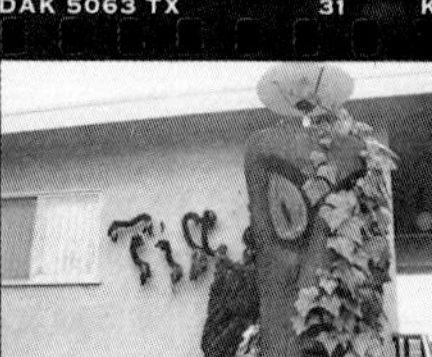

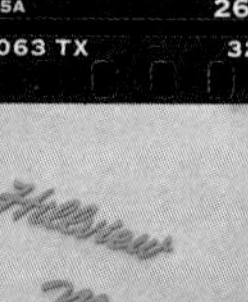

THE
Artesian
WEST
HEATED POOL
EGYPTIAN

EGYPTIAN

EGYPTIAN

HI-LIFE

AMERICANA

714 960-1175
Chez Oro
8234
8248

IL POMPEII

The
PARK WINONA
1840

Seventeen
Twenty
Five

Coral Reef
1736

THE
Hollywood
CAPRI

The
Mariposa

Twin
Palms

THE
Kenmore
CAPRI

THE
Kenmore

Desert Palms

The
Edgemont Capri
1743

The Chalet / "Ok" Chalet

The Oxee Apts / The Ox-Bev Apts

Picadilly Arms / Parliament House

Egyptian / Egyptian

Croft Towers Apts. / The Laguna Deluxe Apartments

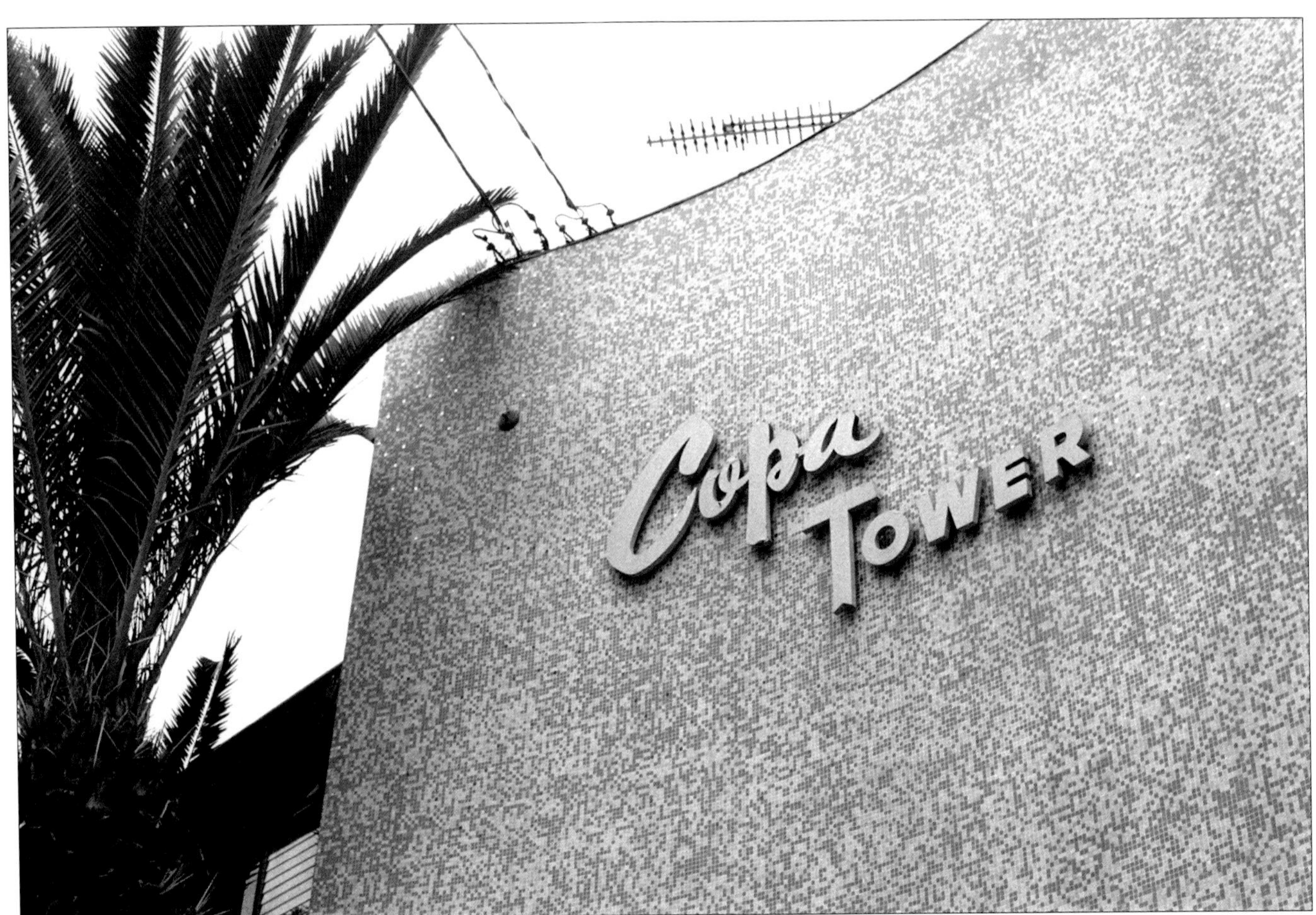

Copa Tower / Copa West

Copa

West

Corbin Continental / Cheviot Capri

Robin / Joanne

The Cinema / The Starlet

Helene Apts. / Helen Towers

The 1823 Apartments / The 824 Apartments

Venice Capri / Venice Villa

The Sun Dial Palms / The Sun Dial Glendon

the
Sun
DiaL
GLENDON

Avalon
Tradewinds

Surf and Sun

Off Shore

El Paseo

Janine
APTS.

Calle Miramar

MARINA MANOR
221

Rivera Tower

Riviera
HOLIDAY
319

Riviera
Villa

Chalet
La Mer

the Palos Verdes
RIVIERA

Tiki

Tiki

SEA SPRAY

STARDUST
STARDUST

WADE MANOR

THE REGENCY

Riviera
12625

VISTA
MANOR
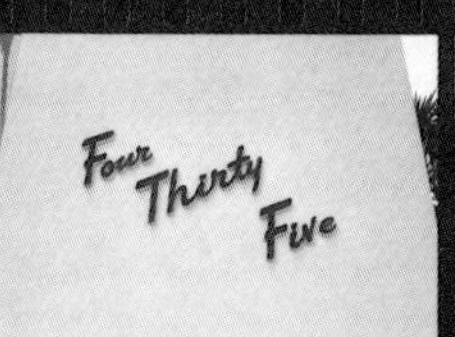
Four
Thirty
Five

the Alexa
500
ST. MORITZ
WILSHIRE
PALACE
Kenmore
TROPICS
Diplomat
1A 2 2A 3 3A 4 4A 5 5A 6 6A 7
K 5063 TX 8 KODAK 5063 TX 9 KODAK 5063 TX 10 KODAK 5063 TX 11 KODAK 5063 TX 12 KODAK 5063 TX 13 KO
The
Loire
THE
CLARIDGE
Four
Twenty
Two
Four
Seventeen
THE Killarney
The
Killarney
324
7A 8 8A 9 9A 10 10A 11 11A 12 12A 13
K 5063 TX 14 KODAK 5063 TX 15 KODAK 5063 TX 16 KODAK 5063 TX 17 KODAK 5063 TX 18 KODAK 5063 TX 19 KO
KENMORE
PALMS
KENMORE
PALMS
334
WILSHIRE CATALINA
the Bachelors
420
Catalina
TROPICS
WILSHIRE BERENDO
333
13A 14 14A 15 15A 16 16A 17 17A 18 18A 19
K 5063 TX 20 KODAK 5063 TX 21 KODAK 5063 TX 22 KODAK 5063 TX 23 KODAK 5063 TX 24 KODAK 5063 TX 25 KO
Apartments
Villa
Riviera
TH
Cameo
APT
The Riviera
Commonwealth
Town House
MI SUEÑO
19A 20 20A 21 21A 22 22A 23 23A 24 24A 25
31 KODAK 5063 TX 32 KODAK 5063 TX 33 KODAK 5063 TX 34 KODAK 5063 TX 35 KODAK 5063 TX 36 KODAK 5063 TX
the
Lorraine
Darby
Dunes
THE
Runnymede
Clark-house
Cavalier Apt.
Villa
Royale

Los Angeles native Lesley Marlene Siegel has been captivated by signage her entire life.

She began her series, "Apartment Living is Great," in the early '90s, as the photographic documentation of Southern California apartment building names, bringing to light their importance in landscape and community history. It now comprises over 2,300 images. The majority of these buildings are affectionately known as "dingbats," boxy '50s and '60s era apartment complexes, their blank façades adorned with the signage that Lesley has been compelled to document over the past eleven years.

By juxtaposing images, using her love of wordplay, her appreciation of graphic design elements and details found on these buildings, Lesley creates thematic groupings: Broadway Musicals, Cinema, Desert, Tiki and Palms are but a few. Curiosity about the stories behind the names led her to create "docu-histories," in which her photographs are combined with text from personal interviews with building owners on how the name came to be, and also include cherished family snapshots. Whenever possible, she salvages actual signs from apartment buildings slated for demolition or renovation.

Some may view dingbat signage as pure kitsch. Not Lesley. She understands and values not only the personal integrity of building owners, but the pairing of their vision with signmaker craftsmanship, having created an abundance of signs using alluring fonts as individual tributes on apartment marquees for all to contemplate.

Lesley began showing her work at the Parker•Zanic Gallery (Los Angeles) in a 1991 show titled *1% - A Group Exhibition of Works for Public Spaces.* Other shows have included: *Urban Scape, Rural Scape at the Downey Museum of Art* (1992); *Crossing LA: Home, Place, Memory* (Los Angeles Festival (1993); and *VeraCITY: Challenging Documentary Views*, curated by the Los Angeles Center for Photographic Studies (1995).

Her work has been featured on *CNN International Headline News* (1994), PBS/KCET's *Visiting With Huell Howser* (1993), in *House Magazine – Simian Issue* (House Industries, 2001), *The Wall Street Journal* (1994), *Los Angeles Times* (1993), *Tiki News* (1995) and Outré Gallery Press's own *Taboo: The Art of Tiki* (1999).

Lesley is excited to be sharing "Apartment Living is Great"– what for her is a special language from the streets of Southern California – by bringing it all the way to Outré Gallery, Melbourne, Australia.

"Apartment Living is Great" by Lesley Marlene Siegel

Published as a limited edition of 1965 hand numbered copies (inclusive of a special edition of 25) in conjunction with the exhibition "Apartment Living is Great", Outré Gallery, Melbourne, 4 July - 22 July, 2003.

ISBN 0 9577684 9 4

Curators: Gemma Jones and Martin McIntosh
Layout & Typesetting: Trevor Slabak
Photo of the artist: Celia Colton Photography

Outré Gallery would like to thank: Lesley Marlene Siegel, Louise Twaddle, Shannon Cane, Trevor Slabak, Kasia Piotrowski, Tom Markovski, John and Lisa Marriot, Miikel Doomernik, Kristine Anstine and Ron Turner at Last Gasp.

For all their individual and endless help, Lesley would like to thank Shirley Siegel and Lewis Siegel, Celia Schwartzman and Laura London, as well as Jack Posnick, Otto von Stroheim, Hilary Cochran, Gerard of Focus Foto, A&I Lab, and acknowledge her extreme gratitude to both Martin McIntosh and Gemma Jones!

Printed in Australia by Brown Prior Anderson, Melbourne

Outré Gallery Press titles are distributed by Last Gasp, 777 Florida, San Francisco, CA 94110, USA

Published by Outré Gallery Press
GPO Box 5442cc, Melbourne, Victoria 3001, AUSTRALIA

About Outré Gallery

Outré Gallery began life in 1998 in a small Melbourne backstreet space to showcase art that wasn't your usual gallery fare. Since its conception Outré Gallery has grown into a larger gallery space and expanded into other ventures including publishing books and prints, feature exhibitions by international artists, tiki mugs and other secret missions.

Our stable of international and local artists include: Shag, Mark Ryden, Tim Biskup, Glenn Barr, Niagara, Coop, Ed "Big Daddy" Roth, Todd Schorr, Bosko, Joe Sorren, Bob Moss, Jeremy Geddes, Gina Garan, Lesley Marlene Siegel, Gemma Jones, Alex Gross, Shepard Fairey and more.

Photographs by Lesley Marlene Siegel are available via our website. Mail order always welcome.
Visit our website at www.outregallery.com

Lesley Manor / The Sea Gull